ONLINE SAFETY

By
Steffi Cavell-Clarke

©2018
Book Life
King's Lynn
Norfolk PE30 4LS

ISBN: 978-1-78637-255-0

Written by:
Steffi Cavell-Clarke

Edited by:
Kirsty Holmes

Designed by:
Gareth Liddington

A catalogue record for this book
is available from the British Library

MANCHESTER
CITY COUNCIL

Please return/renew this item
by the last date shown.
Books may also be renewed by
phone or the internet.

Tel: 0161 254 7777

www.manchester.gov.uk/libraries

ONLINE SAFETY

Words that look like **this** can be found in the glossary on page 24.

Using a Computer

A computer is a type of **machine**. Computers are used all around the world and they can help you to do many different things.

Computers can help us do lots of things, like drawing pictures, writing stories, playing music and learning new things. They are very useful.

"I love to watch videos on my tablet computer."

Ashley – aged 6

Going Online

Being 'online' means that you are using the Internet. The Internet is a **network** of lots and lots of computers that are connected to each other.

"I use the Internet to speak to my friend who lives very far away."

Thomas – aged 5

You can use the Internet on computers, tablets and smartphones. You might use it to play games or chat to friends.

Being Safe Online

Just like in real life, you need to make sure that you are safe when you are using the Internet.

The most important thing you can do to stay safe online is to make sure that your parents or carers know that you are using the Internet.

Security and Passwords

Passwords are words that you choose, and keep secret, to allow you to unlock a computer so you can use it. Passwords keep our computers **secure** and stop other people using them.

Username   user

Password   *******

Login

"I would never tell my friends my password because it is private."

Rebecca – aged 7

Try not to use things like the names of pets or friends for your password. You should use a mix of letters and numbers to make sure no one can guess what it is.

Sharing Personal Information

Personal information tells other people who you are and where to find you. Personal information includes your name, address, school and what you look like. You should not share this kind of information with people you do not know.

Never **post** anything on the Internet that you wouldn't want the world to see. Once something is posted online, it may become impossible to remove.

Using Social Media

People use social media to **communicate** with other people from all around the world. Facebook, Twitter, Instagram and Snapchat are all types of social media.

You can use social media to share information, photos and videos with your friends and family. Make sure that you keep your social media **accounts** private, so **strangers** cannot see what you are sharing.

Making Friends Online

The friendships you make online can seem very real, but they are not the same as the friendships you make in day-to-day life.

We usually cannot see who we are talking to over the Internet. This means that it can be hard to tell if a person is who they say they are.

"An online friend asked to meet up with me. I asked my dad if it was OK and he explained that I didn't really know who my friend was and that it might not be safe."

Richard – aged 8

Cyberbullying

Cyberbullying is where someone uses the Internet to hurt, scare, or embarrass other people. Sharing private photos, posting nasty comments and sending hurtful messages are all examples of cyberbullying.

"My sister posted a photo of me I didn't like on Facebook. I told our mum and she told her to remove it."

Jessica – aged 6

People cyberbully because it's easier to be nasty to someone from behind a computer screen than in real-life. All forms of bullying are unacceptable.

Asking for Help

If you see anything online that upsets you, or makes you feel that you are not safe, tell a grown-up who you can trust straight away.

Just like in the real world, people online can do or say things that upset you. Talk to a **responsible** adult who can help you be safe online.

Top Tips for Online Safety

Think Before You Post

Don't upload or share anything you wouldn't want your parents, teachers or friends to see.

Think About New People

Remember that not everyone online can be trusted. Never meet up with online friends, unless you take a responsible adult with you.

Think Before You Share

Never share your personal information, like your address or telephone number, with people you don't know.

GLOSSARY

accounts	the parts of a website that only you can access
communicate	pass information between two or more people
machine	a tool or device that can do a job
network	a system of connected people or things
post	upload something online
responsible	trusted to do the right thing
strangers	people you do not know
secure	safe

INDEX